The Magic of Music

9 Imaginative Solos for Early Intermediate Pianists

Dennis Alexander

Foreword

I've always felt that music inspires magic. Everyone who experiences the joy of making some kind of music develops the ability to discover this magic in one way or another. Perhaps it is that special feeling which occurs when a certain rhythm or colorful harmony touches the heart of the player. Or maybe it is that favorite melodic line which inspires one to "sing inside" and feel the warmth of a beautifully turned phrase. The pieces in this collection are designed to entertain, reinforce and enhance the important musical and technical skills which are being developed at the early intermediate level. Whether it is the gentle blending of fall colors in "Autumn Haze," the robust energy of "Gypsy Fire" or the rollicking rhythms of "Turtle Rock Rag," students will develop their own magical imagination through the repertoire that is contained in this collection! I wish you much success and enjoyment as you journey through "The Magic of Music."

Dennis Alexander

Contents

This collection is dedicated to my friend and colleague, Mary Ellen Cavelti.

Autumn Haze

Dennis Alexander

Andante cantabile

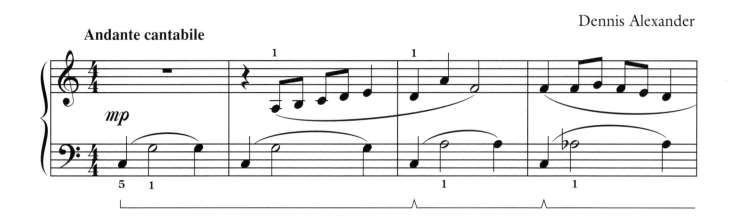

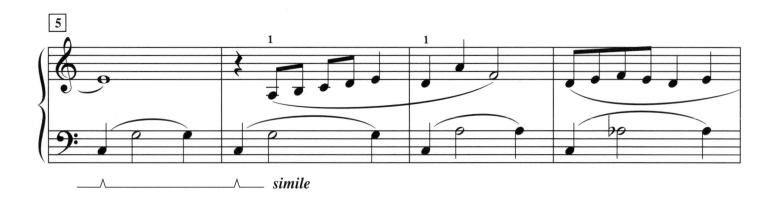

simile

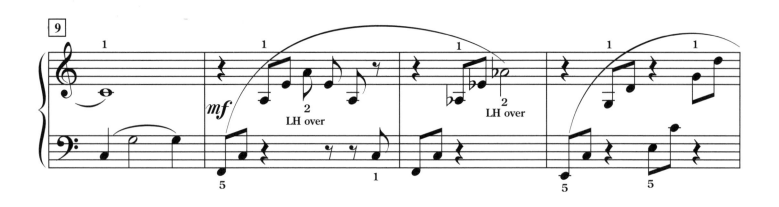

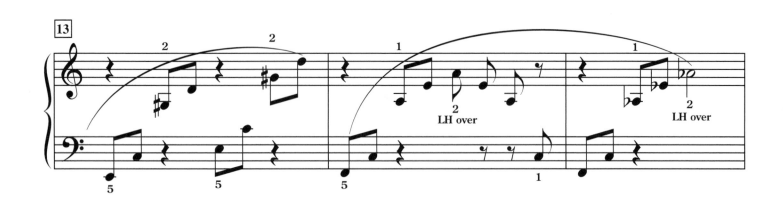

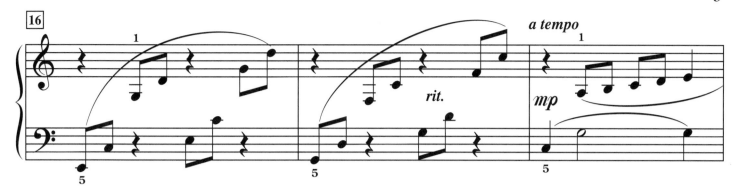

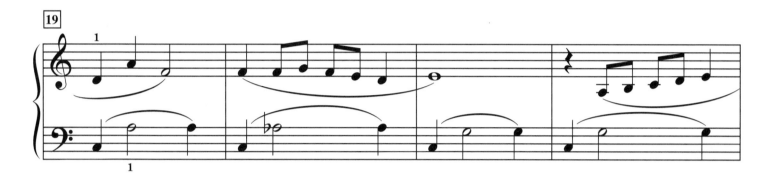

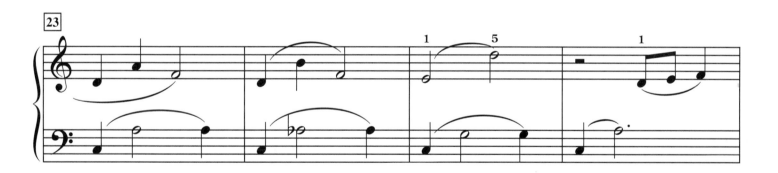

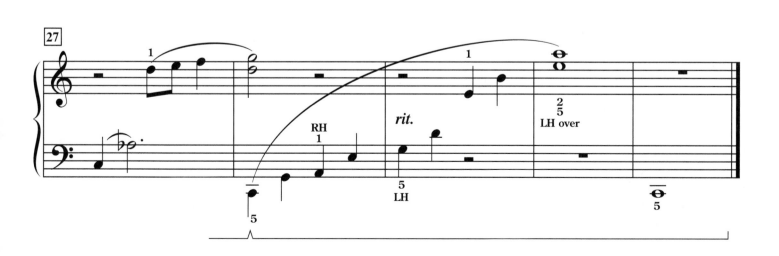

La Valse

Dennis Alexander

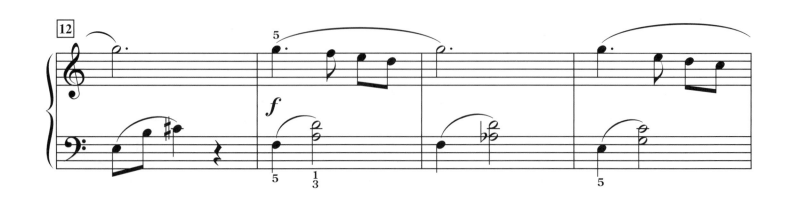

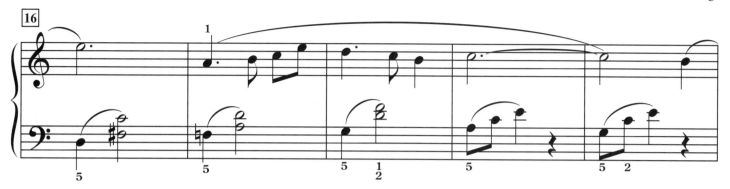

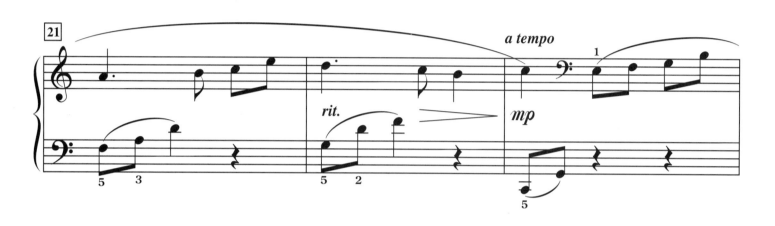

Gypsy Fire!

Dennis Alexander

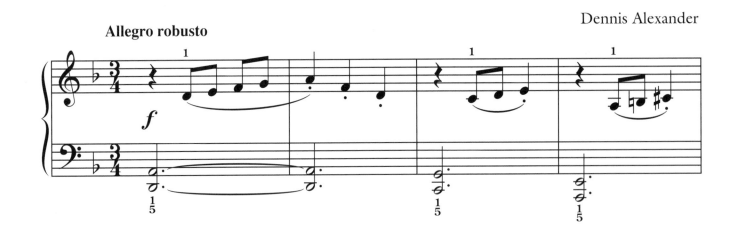

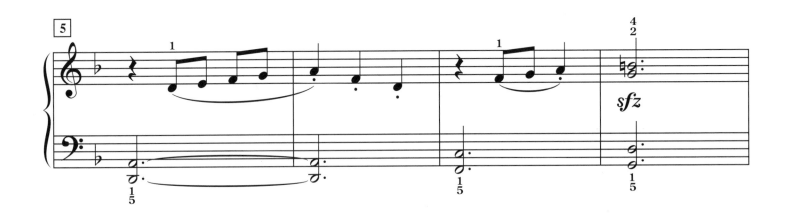

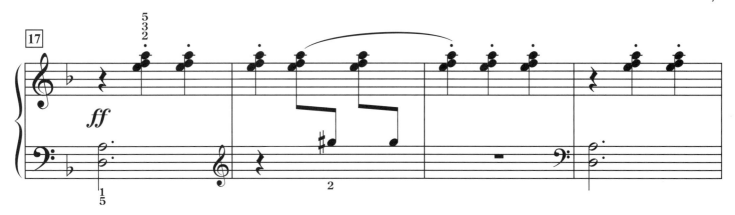

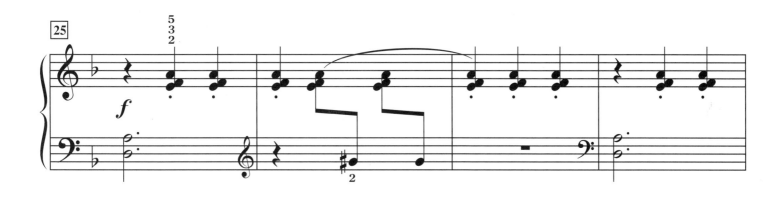

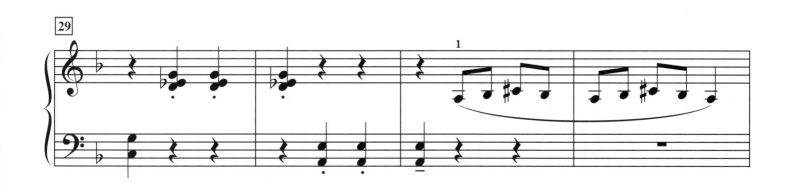

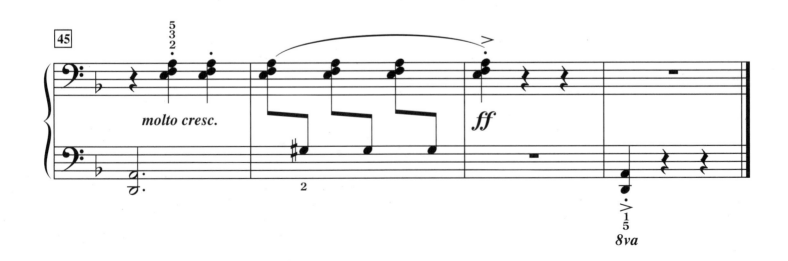

Heather

Dennis Alexander

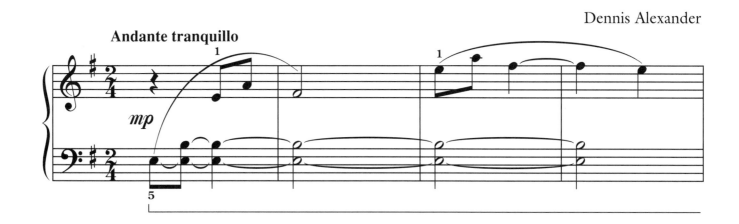

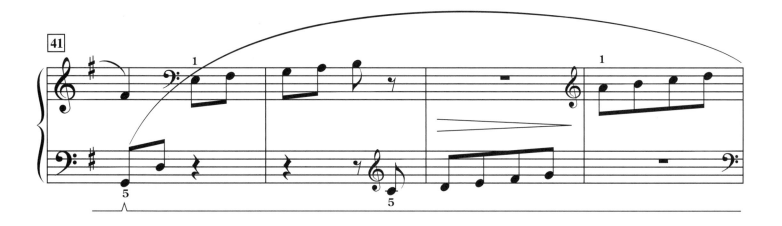

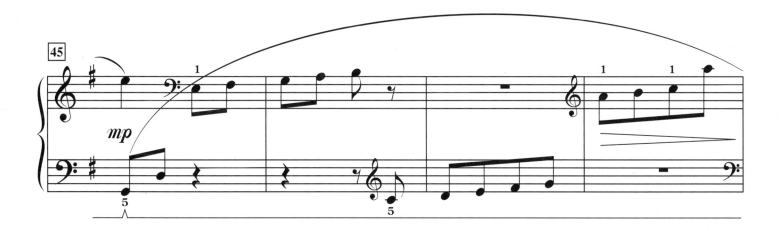

High Steppers!

Dennis Alexander

Allegro energico

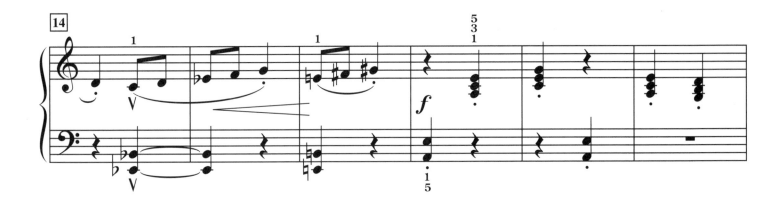

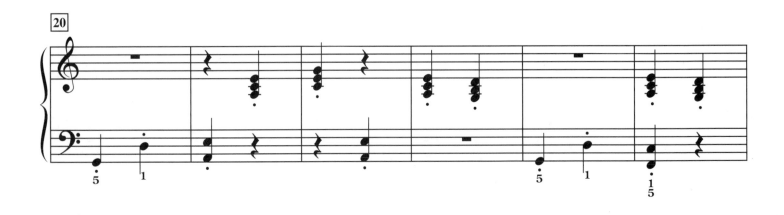

Preludium

Dennis Alexander

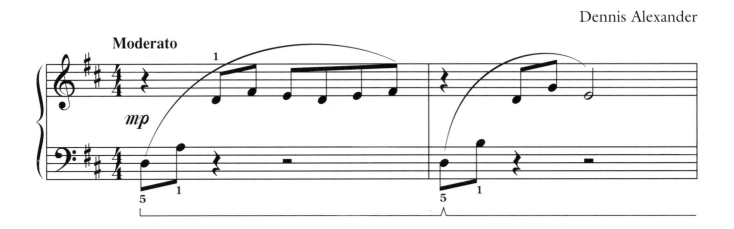

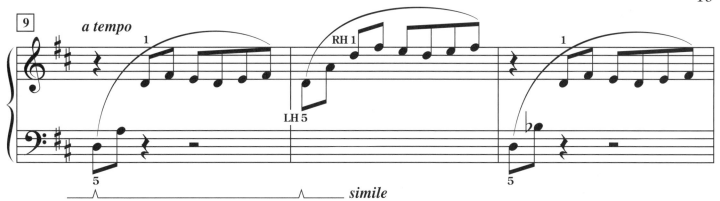

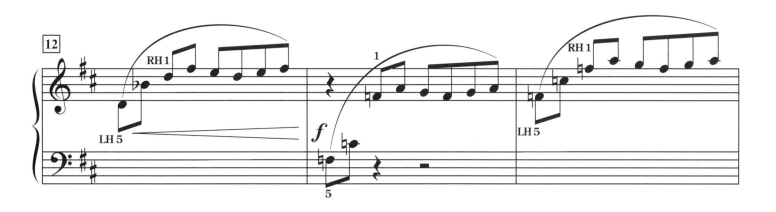

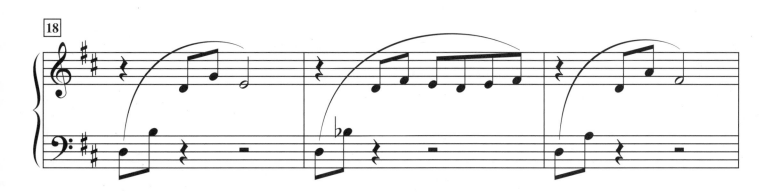

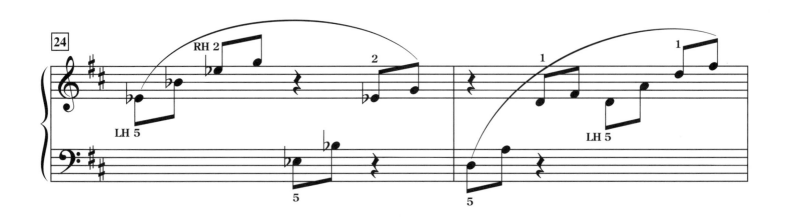

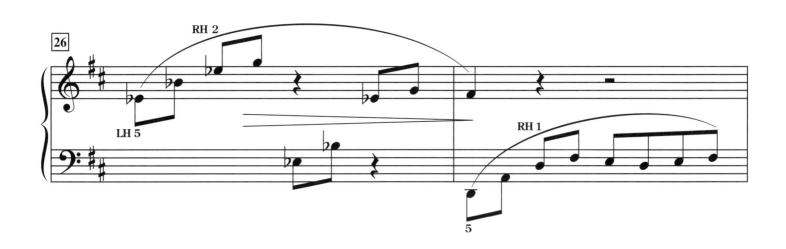

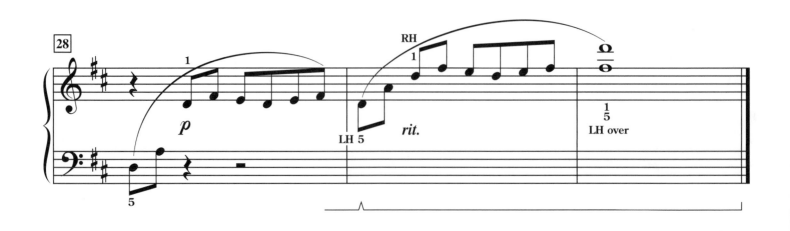

Turtle Rock Rag

Dennis Alexander

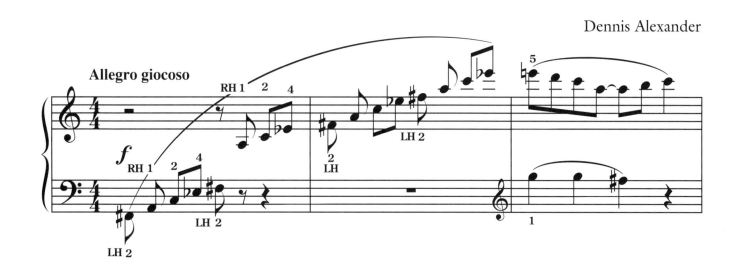

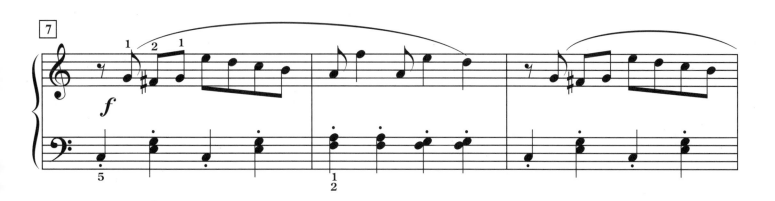

The Sad Troubador

Dennis Alexander

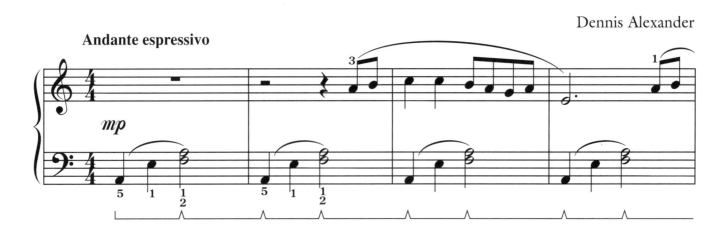

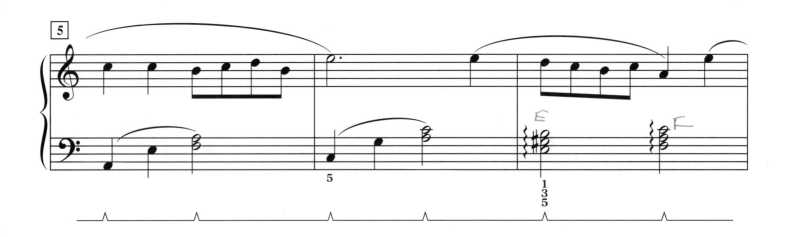

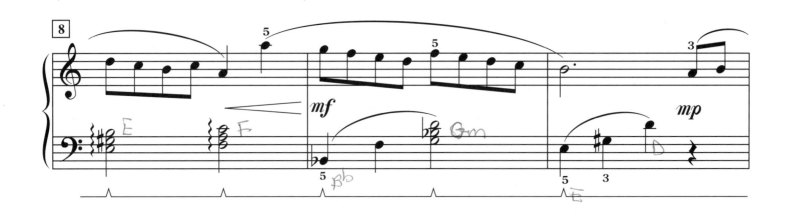

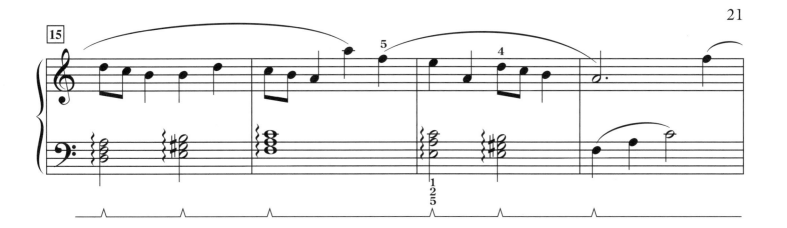

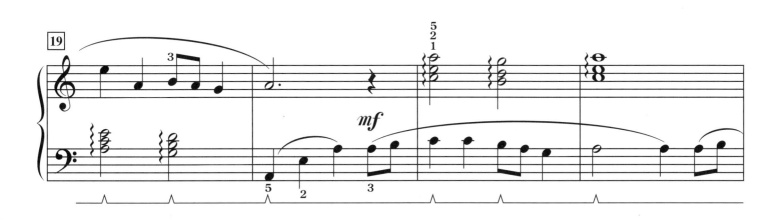

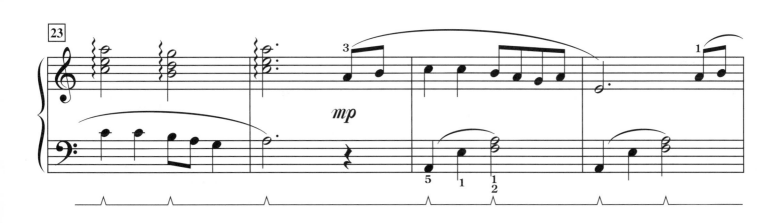

Fiddle-i-o

Dennis Alexander

Allegro scherzando

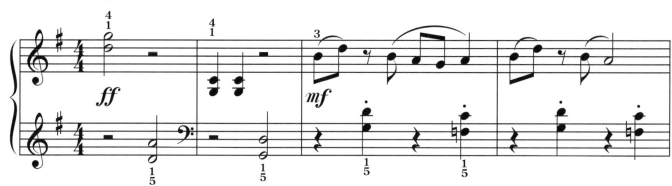

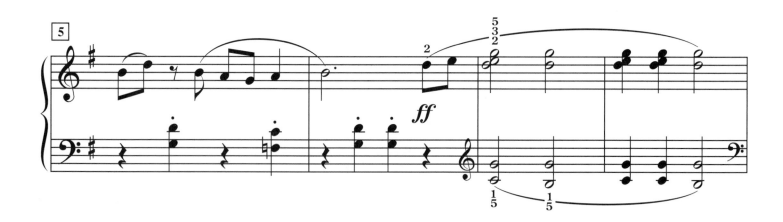

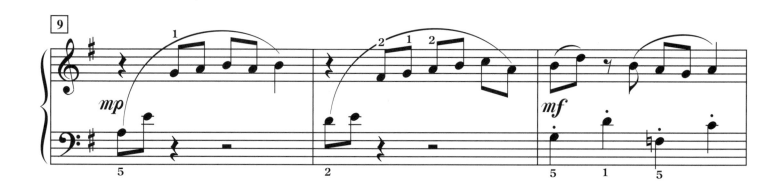

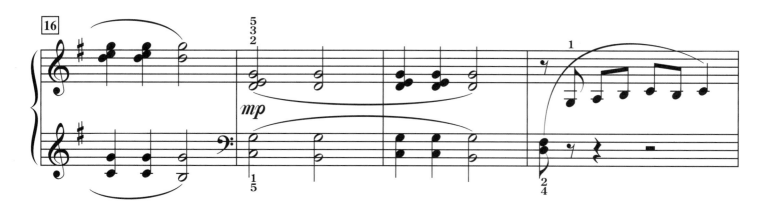